Estl

GW00994415

THE BRAVE QUEEN

The Story of Esther
accurately retold from the Bible
(from the book of Esther), by
CARINE MACKENZIE

Design and Illustrations
Duncan McLaren

Published in Great Britain by
CHRISTIAN FOCUS PUBLICATIONS LTD
Geanies House, Fearn, Tain, Ross-shire IV20 1TW, Scotland
http://www.christianfocus.com
© 1988 Christian Focus Publications Ltd ISBN 0 906731 64 X

printed   1992
Reprinted 1998
Reprinted 2000

03412

Esther was a very beautiful Jewish girl. Her people had been taken away by force from their own land, so Esther lived in the land of

Persia which today we call Iran.
Esther's mother and father were
both dead and she had been
brought up by her uncle's son, a
kind man called Mordecai.

Ruling over Persia was the mighty king Ahasuerus. He had a wonderful palace in Shushan, with white, green and blue curtains, fastened with silver rings to marble pillars and rich marble floors coloured red, blue, white and black.

Ahasuerus made a grand feast for all his princes and servants. There was plenty of food and drink. After seven days of eating and drinking, the king gave the order that Vashti the queen was to come from her rooms in the palace, into the dining hall so that all the princes could admire her beauty.

"Tell the king, I will not come," said Vashti. King Ahasuerus was very angry with her. He and his advisers decided to punish Vashti. She was to be queen no longer. Someone else was to be chosen to take her place.

A notice was sent out through the land. Any beautiful young girl who would like to become queen should come to the palace in Shushan. The king would choose the one he liked best.

Many girls flocked to the royal palace and among them was Esther. She spent a whole year in the palace preparing to meet the king. Every day Mordecai walked past the courtyard of Esther's house, to find out if all was well.

Eventually it was Esther's turn to
go to the king. When he saw her,
he loved her more then anyone
else. He put the royal crown on
her head and made her the queen,
instead of Vashti. He made a great
feast in her honour. But no-one in
the palace knew that she was a
Jewish girl. Mordecai had thought
it wiser that she kept that secret.
Esther did as Mordecai asked.

One day Mordecai overheard two of the king's officers plotting to kill king Ahasuerus. Mordecai told Esther and she reported it to the king giving Mordecai the credit. The report was investigated and found to be quite true. Both men were hanged. The whole story was written in the royal record books.

The most important person in the king's service was a proud man called Haman. Everytime he passed by, the people would bow down to him — everyone except Mordecai. Mordecai was a Jew, who bowed down only to God. We too must worship only God and not allow anyone or anything else to take His place. Haman was enraged by this insult. He was so angry he wanted to get rid of all the Jews from the land, especially Mordecai.

Wicked Haman made up a law
that every Jewish person
throughout the land, young and
old, men, women and children,
would be killed on a certain day,
eleven months later. The king
agreed to the law and copies of it
were sent throughout the land.

Mordecai heard the terrible news. He put on coarse, rough garments instead of his own clothes and put ashes on his head to show how sad he was. He cried loudly and bitterly.

News was brought to Esther that her cousin was sitting outside the gate in a sorry state. Esther was very upset. She sent out some nice new clothes to Mordecai but he refused to take them.

Esther sent Hatach, her special servant, to find out what was Mordecai's problem. Mordecai told him all about Haman's wicked plot. He gave a copy of the law for Esther to see for herself.

"Perhaps Esther can plead with the king on behalf of her people," said Mordecai. "How can I do that?" thought Esther. "No-one is allowed to go into the king's presence, without being asked. He has not asked me for the last thirty days".

Mordecai urged Esther to think of something. "You would be killed too," he said.

"Who knows, but you may have been made queen so that you could do something now."

God had Esther's life in His plan. He knew each step. God has your life in His plan too. Everything is known to Him.

Esther sent back her reply to Mordecai. "Gather all the Jews in the town of Shushan and fast for three days. I and my maids will do the same. Then I will go to see the king. And if I die, I die."

But Esther did not die. When she went to see the king, three days later, he was pleased to see her. He held out his golden sceptre, which was a sign that she could come near him.

How amazing to think that we can speak to the King of Kings at any time. We can pray to God and tell Him our problems and He will listen to us and help us.

"What do you want, queen Esther?" asked Ahasuerus. "You can have anything you wish, even half of my kingdom."

"I would like you and Haman to come to a banquet today," replied Esther.

"Certainly," said the king. "Tell Haman to hurry to a banquet prepared by Esther," he ordered.

Esther did not tell the king yet of her problem. At the feast, he again asked her what she would like from him. Perhaps she felt the time was not right or perhaps she was afraid.

She said, "I would like the king
and Haman to come to another
banquet tomorrow."

Haman was highly delighted with this special honour. The only thing that spoiled his enjoyment was the sight of Mordecai at the king's gate, standing straight and tall as he went past. Mordecai would not bow down to him. When Haman went home he boasted to his wife and family of how favoured he was by the king and queen Esther. "But all these honours are worth nothing to me, so long as I see that Jew Mordecai."

"You should get rid of Mordecai," they all suggested. "Build a big gallows seventy-five feet high and have Mordecai hanged."

"What a good idea," thought Haman. "I will do that straight away." What a wicked man Haman was. But things did not work out as Haman had expected. God's timing is perfect. He has all His creatures and all their actions, in His care.

That night the king could not sleep. "Bring a book and read it to me," he ordered. One of the record books was brought and the story of how Mordecai had uncovered the plot to kill Ahasuerus was read out. The king was very interested to hear this. "What honour has been done to Mordecai to show my gratitude?" "Nothing has been done," he was told.

"Something must be done right away. Is there any official about at this time of night?"

Ahasuerus was told that Haman was there. "Good, bring him to me, at once," the king said.

"Haman, I want to honour someone. What would be the best way to do that?" asked the king.

"Oh," thought Haman. "Surely he means to honour me."

"Well," said Haman. "A good idea would be to let the man wear your royal robes and royal crown and be led on your horse through the city streets."

"Hurry up and do just that to Mordecai, the Jew, who sits at my gate."

Haman was shocked. How horrified he felt giving this honour to the man he hated so much.

While he was telling his wife and friends of his misfortune, he was hastily called to Esther's second banquet.

Esther entertained the king and the wicked Haman at another lovely meal. The king asked her again, "What can I do for you?"

"Oh King," replied Esther. "Please spare my life and the lives of my people. A plot has been hatched to kill all the Jewish people. If we were only to be sold as slaves, I would have held my tongue."

"Who has decided to do this?" demanded Ahasuerus.

"This wicked man Haman," declared Esther.

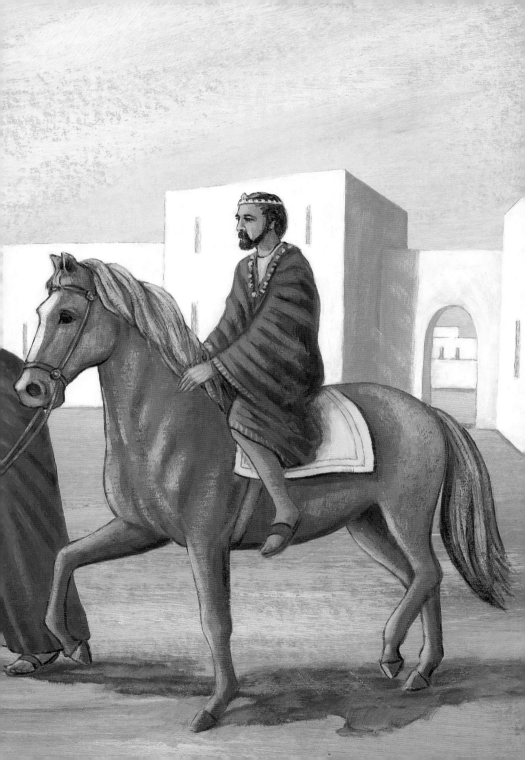

Haman was terrified. The king was so angry, he went out into the palace garden. Haman turned to Esther and begged her to be lenient with him, but the king was enraged as he thought Haman

was trying to hurt Esther.

"Haman has made gallows to hang Mordecai on," the king was told. "Hang Haman on them instead," he ordered.

King Ahasuerus gave Haman's
property and lands to Esther.
Esther told the king that Mordecai
was her cousin. Mordecai was
given Haman's ring and Esther

made Mordecai the manager of Haman's estate.

Esther begged the king to reverse the orders that Haman had sent round the country.

So the royal scribes were called to write another letter to be sent to all the corners of the kingdom. The letter was sealed with the king's ring and sent out by messengers on fast horses, or mules, or young camels.

The Jews were to have power over the other people in the land instead of being subject to them.

Mordecai was highly honoured by the king. He was given a blue and white robe and a crown of gold. He was next in importance to the king.

The Jewish people were very glad
and had many celebration feasts
and sent presents to one another.

What Esther did is still
remembered by Jews to this day.

But what God did for them is even more important. He has the lives of all men in His hand. What we sometimes think is chance, is really God's providence working.

The Bible tells us that "ALL THINGS work together for good to them that love God."